Kings of the Wild

Contents

Brown bear country 2

What do brown bears look like? 4

Where do brown bears live? 10

What do brown bears eat? 14

How do brown bears live? 18

Why do bears fight? 20

How do brown bears "talk" to each other? 24

An Alaskan brown bear's year 26

The brown bear in danger 40

Saving brown bears 43

Glossary 44

Index 45

A brown bear's year 46

Written and photographed by Jonathan and Angela Scott

Collins

Brown bear country

Welcome to brown bear country. Brown bears are some of the largest meat-eating animals on Earth, and carve out a life in the rocky shorelines, mountains and forests in the most northern countries of the globe. In these conditions brown bears have to be tough, strong animals to survive.

What do brown bears look like?

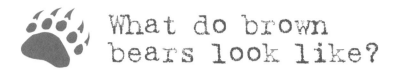

Brown bears can be all different colours of brown from almost cream or golden to darkest chocolate. Their fur can sometimes look frosted with tips of white or tan and in North America, if they are living inland, they are often called grizzly bears.

4

hump

angular face

Whatever their colour, you can spot them because their large, well-developed shoulder muscles form a hump on their shoulders and their faces aren't as round as those of black bears.

How big are brown bears?

This table shows how big brown bears can grow compared to other meat-eaters:

Animal	Length (head to rump)	Height (at shoulder)
brown bear	280 cm	150 cm
tiger	280 cm	110 cm
lion	190 cm	110 cm
grey wolf	160 cm	100 cm

Polar bears are the largest bears, but brown bears are also very large. A male brown bear can stand over three metres high and weigh 600 kilograms or more. That's as much as six or seven grown men. Female bears are smaller than male bears.
The biggest brown bears live along the coast in Alaska.

Brown bears often stand upright on two legs. Sometimes it's because they're curious and want to see what's going on, and sometimes it's because they want to reach higher up a tree for food. They also do this to threaten other animals.

Brown bears are very powerful animals. They can climb and swim and they are especially good at digging holes. But in spite of their size, they can also run fast – they can chase and catch a deer running at 50 kilometres per hour.

Bears can't draw in their front claws, which are often as much as 12 centimetres long. Their back claws are only half that length. They often use their great forepaws like hands to feed themselves.

These bear paw-prints are bigger than a man's hand.

Bears can sniff out food from far away, even when it's locked inside cars. They also have very good hearing and eyesight. Bears can see in colour unlike dogs, which are related to them. This is probably to help them know which berries and shoots are good to eat.

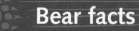

Bears have a very good sense of smell and can sniff out food from far away.

Where do brown bears live?

Brown bears live in some of the wildest places on Earth. They've learnt to survive in forest areas where they can easily hide, river valleys where there's plenty of food, grassy meadows and on remote coasts.

They also live on the cold northern plains south of the Arctic circle. A few bears still remain in the mountains of Europe and Asia, but today they mostly live in Canada, Alaska or Russia.

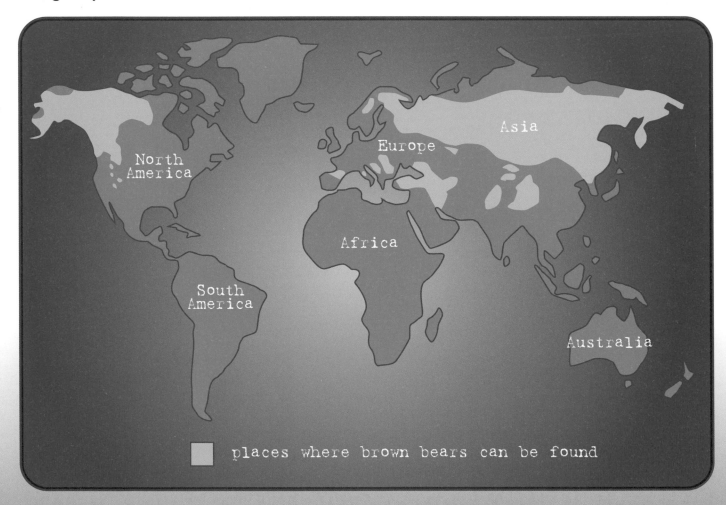

North America

South America

Europe

Asia

Africa

Australia

■ places where brown bears can be found

Brown bears can
live in meadows.

Brown bears can also live beside
rivers, or among mountains.

There are eight different kinds of bear found around the world.

polar bear

brown bear

North American black bear

Asiatic black bear

sun bear

sloth bear

spectacled bear

giant panda

Modern brown bears are closely related to black bears and polar bears. Scientists think that thousands of years ago during the Ice Age, some brown bears ended up living in the far north. They survived by eating seals, and over hundreds of thousands of years they developed into polar bears.

Brown bears are found in a greater variety of places than any other kind of bear.

What do brown bears eat?

The answer is – almost everything! Bears are very clever and inventive, especially if there's a meal to be had.

More than three quarters of their food is vegetarian, and what they can find to eat depends on the time of year. However they'll also rip open a log to get at the tasty grubs inside, scavenge from another animal, or make a kill of their own.

Often they'll hide food, burying it under leaves or sand. It's very dangerous to approach a bear guarding a food store. Nothing can take food away from them – except another bear.

Bear facts

Bears are **omnivores**. This means they eat meat, fish and vegetables, including shellfish, seaweed, mushrooms, grass, insects and birds' eggs.

On the coast, brown bears can often be seen at low tide digging up juicy clams to eat. They scoop the clams into their mouths, and crack open the shells with their powerful jaws. Then they spit out the broken shell onto the back of one of their giant forepaws and slurp up the tasty shellfish.

Bears steal the eggs of sea birds even if they have to swim ten kilometres to reach the islands where they live. They search the shoreline for dead fish or other food brought in by the tide.

How do brown bears live?

Brown bears may look scary but they're actually rather shy creatures. Unless they're hurt, or defending their cubs or their food, they rarely attack humans.

However bears who live on open plains, where there are fewer places to hide, are more likely to have to defend themselves.

Most bears, including mothers with cubs, live on their own in a huge area of land that they know well, and they'll travel as much as 65 kilometres in a day in search of food. But sometimes, if the weather is hot and they aren't hunting, they'll scrape out a comfortable day-bed on the ground hidden in the bushes. If there are no humans or other bears around, they may even make it in the open and snooze through the long hot afternoon.

a brown bear dozing in the sun

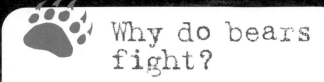

Why do bears fight?

Brown bears usually live alone, but if they meet another bear, each will want to show the other that they're the strongest and claim the right to the best food and the safest shelter. This is especially true if they're both males, although females will fight too. The two animals will often rear up on their hind legs and show their teeth. Each animal will try to frighten the other into giving way, but they both know that it would be very dangerous to run at that point. If one bear turns its back to the other, it may be run down and killed straight away.

If neither bear backs down, they'll bite, wrestle and swat each other with their huge paws until one bear is the winner. Then the defeated bear will slink away as quietly as it can.

At certain times of the year, when there's plenty of food in one spot, the bears come together and then a pecking order develops. Each bear must find its own space. Usually all the bears give way to the biggest males, but if cubs are in danger, their mothers will stand up against anyone.

These are **sedge** meadows, where the bears gather to eat new grass.

22

A bear will hide
food to eat later.

The ripe berry fields
mean food for bears.

23

How do brown bears "talk" to each other?

Bears are quiet animals, but they can make themselves understood.

Cubs whimper and squeal to get their mother's attention. They also make a contented humming sound when they're feeding from their mother.

When adult bears are alarmed, they make a strange noise with their mouth, called "jaw popping". It sounds a little like a cork coming out of a bottle. Mother bears often do this to warn their cubs of danger. They also make huffing and puffing sounds.

When two adult bears threaten each other, they growl, snarl and roar.

An Alaskan brown bear's year

Winter: the long sleep

A bear's life is ruled by the seasons. Throughout spring, summer and autumn it hunts continually for food, in order to grow a thick layer of fat mainly around its hindquarters.

In October and November, as winter approaches, the shorter days warn the bear that it must get ready for the long months ahead without food or water. Now it must find a safe place to sleep.

European bears like to find a cave or a hollow tree.
North American brown bears usually dig a new den each year,
as the old one often collapses in the spring rains.

The den
A single tunnel about one or
two metres long leads to an
egg-shaped room about a metre high
and one or two metres across.
It's often lined with grass.

sleeping
chamber

entrance

tunnel

moss and grass
for lining

When the bear goes into its den, it curls up and falls into a light sleep. Its heart beats more slowly and its whole body slows down, rather like a machine on standby. It doesn't need to eat or drink or go to the toilet. This is called hibernation.

Bear facts

When it hibernates, a bear's heartbeat slows from about 40 beats per minute to about eight.

Hibernation is the bear's way of coping with the long winter months, when there's nothing for it to eat. While it sleeps, its body slowly uses up most of the food it stored earlier as fat. Because it isn't doing much, except breathing very lightly, the bear can hibernate for a long time before it needs to eat again. Strangely enough, the bear can wake up quickly if it's in danger, but it may hibernate for as long as six months.

Bear facts

Some bears will lose as much as half their weight by spring.

Bear facts

Bears need a layer of fat five centimetres thick to see them through the winter.

29

Midwinter: the cubs are born

Baby cubs are born at the beginning of January. The mother bear gives birth to two or three tiny cubs, which will live off their mother's milk in the warm safety of the den. Amazingly, the mother bear won't give birth to cubs unless she has enough fat to keep her alive throughout the winter. This means that only cubs with a good chance of survival are born. If the mother bear dies, her cubs will not be able to live without her.

Bear facts

Bear cubs weigh less than half a kilogram when they're born. They're blind and almost hairless.

A mother bear and her cubs usually leave their den later than other bears, around the middle of May. This is because earlier in the spring, there isn't much food and there are many hungry animals about, including other bears and wolves. However, even in May, leaving the den is still a very dangerous time for baby bears, and nearly half of all cubs do not survive.

The cubs get bigger very quickly. They may already weigh over five kilograms when they come out of their den, but they stay very close to their mother.

Mother bears are extremely dangerous if they feel their cubs are threatened. A mother bear will fight for her cubs more fiercely than almost any other animal.

Most cubs leave their mothers when they're about two years old, but some stay another year. Young bears often can't get enough food to survive the winter on their own and they are in danger from other bears.

a mother bear with her cubs

By the time they're seven or eight years old, female bears are fully grown and may have cubs of their own.

Bear facts

A female bear will only have cubs every two to three years, because she needs to give them all her care. Over her lifetime, she'll be unlikely to raise more than ten cubs safely to **independence**.

Spring and summer

Like all brown bears, newly independent cubs feed on the sedge grass in the spring meadows. They must now start the serious business of putting on weight if they are to survive the next winter.

Young bears love to play-fight.

In late June or July in Alaska, the first salmon arrive on their way to lay their eggs upstream. The fish arrive in tens of thousands and the bears gather by the rivers to feast. This is one of the reasons why the brown bears on the coast grow so big.

Feeding on the salmon

Bears find their own spaces to fish and feed, but the strongest bears usually claim the best spots.

They catch the fish in different ways. Some drive the salmon into the shallow water where they can hook them out with their claws. Some swim in the river and catch them in their open mouths.

An experienced bear can catch up to 20 salmon in an hour.

Once it has caught a fish, a bear may choose to sneak away with its prize. Bears like to eat the salmon's skin, head and eggs most of all, because these provide the most fat.

Getting in shape for winter

The salmon continue to arrive throughout the summer until the middle of September. By then, the berries and nuts are ripe. At this point, the bigger bears can be eating as much as 40 kilograms of food a day and putting on two to three kilograms in weight every 24 hours.

It doesn't matter to the bears that they can no longer move as quickly as they did in the spring. They don't fear any animals except other bears.

Bear facts

Bears put on fat around their hips and thighs. When they're ready to hibernate they're so fat, they almost seem to waddle.

39

The brown bear in danger

People have always respected and admired bears, and bears feature in the earliest North American cave paintings. Perhaps this is because bears seem a bit like humans. They can stand up on two feet, and they use their big forepaws like hands.

But sadly, out of the eight different kinds of bear, six are in danger.

tourists photographing a
bear in the wild

Over the last hundred years, brown bears have disappeared from many parts of the world. This is because, although brown bears are big and strong, their way of life is very fragile and easily destroyed. They depend on huge areas of **wilderness** where they can find large amounts of fresh food. They're especially sensitive to **pollution**.

Bears are most in danger from people who want to use the wilderness where the bears live for logging and farming, or to get oil or minerals. Some people also like hunting bears for sport.

When people move into an area, bears are tempted to attack livestock or scavenge food from rubbish and even people's homes. This way, humans and bears become enemies. But in North America, people are trying to work on these problems and to make sure that the brown bear is left alone. In some places, it's against the law to hunt them and the number of roads built through their land is strictly controlled.

Bear facts

In Yellowstone, North West Wyoming, USA, in 1975, there were only about 200 brown bears left in the wild. By 2005, there were nearly 600.

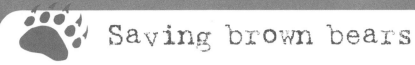

Saving brown bears

Brown bears need a great deal of living space. They can't survive without their wilderness. It's important for us to find ways of using this land without destroying it for the animals that live there.

For this reason, scientists are now learning as much as they can about brown bears. They're studying how they live to find out how to keep these kings of the wild safe for the future.

43

Glossary

den	a tunnel, cave or hollow tree, where a bear spends the winter
hibernation	a special sleep that bears and other animals fall into during the winter, to help them survive when food is scarce
independence	ability to survive without help and protection
inventive	clever, imaginative, with lots of ideas
omnivores	animals that eat anything – meat, fish, fruit and vegetables
pecking order	the order of power and importance among members of a group
pollution	damage caused by manmade chemicals
scavenge	take food that other animals or people have abandoned or thrown away
sedge	plants that grow in wet ground, sometimes near rivers
survival	staying alive
wilderness	wild and remote country, without roads or buildings

Index

age   9

appearance   4, 5, 6

black bears   5, 12, 13

claws   8

colour   4

cubs   18, 22, 24, 25, 30, 31, 32, 33, 34

day-bed   19

den   27, 30, 31, 32

endangered   40, 41, 42, 43

fighting   18, 20, 21, 32

food   14, 15, 16, 17, 26, 28, 34, 35, 36, 37, 38

hibernation   28, 29, 39

home   2, 10, 11, 41, 42, 43

noises   24, 25

pecking order   22

polar bears   6, 12, 13

salmon   35, 36, 37, 38

senses   9

speed   8

standing upright   6, 7

types of bear   12

weight   (adult) 6, (cubs) 31

A brown bear's year

Spring

The mother brown bear comes out of her den after her long winter sleep with her cubs. She's hungry and she needs to eat and drink.

Winter

The weather is colder and there isn't much food, but most of the brown bears have enough fat to keep them safely through the winter. It's time for the bears to hibernate in their winter dens. The cubs will be born at the beginning of January.

Summer

This is a time of plenty for the brown bears and they especially love to eat fresh salmon.
They must eat as much as they can to put on a layer of fat.

Autumn

There's still a lot of food for the brown bears, but finding it is often hard for the younger bears.
They don't have the chance to get as much food as the stronger ones.

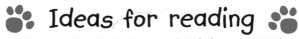# Ideas for reading

Written by Linda Pagett B.Ed (hons), M.Ed
Lecturer and Educational Consultant

Reading objectives:
- predict what might happen from details stated and implied
- listen to and discuss non-fiction and reference books
- read exception words, noting the unusual correspondences between spelling and sound, and where these occur in the word
- retrieve and record information from non-fiction
- identify main ideas drawn from more than one paragraph and summarise these

Spoken language objectives:
- give well-structured descriptions, explanations and narratives for different purposes
- use relevant strategies to build their vocabulary
- maintain attention and participate actively in collaborative conversations, staying on topic and initiating and responding to comments

Curriculum links: Geography; ICT

Interest words: hibernation, omnivores, pecking order, scavenge, sedge

Resources: computer

Build a context for reading

This book can be read over two or more reading sessions.

- Read the title and blurb together in order to decide the purpose of the book.
- Look at the contents page together and consider four questions: *What do brown bears look like? Where do brown bears live? What do brown bears eat? How do brown bears live?*
- Ask the children what they think answers might be.
- Scan through the pictures and text of those chapters together and decide if their predictions were right.

Understand and apply reading strategies

- Leaf through the rest of the book together and decide what makes the book interesting (e.g. *pictures, captions*). Let the pictures lead their interest in researching different aspects of the book (e.g. *cubs*).
- Scan through the glossary to make sure the children understand new vocabulary and concepts.
- Allow the children time to read through the book independently.

Develop reading and language comprehension

- Write the words *bear* and *bare* on whiteboard. Investigate other homophones (e.g. *key, quay*).